This book belongs to:

_____

_____

Other books by Ally's Mum:

Ally Makes a New Friend
Let's Get Dressed!
Let's go to the Airport!
Let's go to the Hairdresser!
Let's Brush our Teeth!

Website:
itsokally.com

Developed by:
Ally's Mum
Mothers & Marketers

Published by Mothers & Marketers
Melbourne, Australia
mothersandmarketers.com

©2023 ItsOkAlly. All rights reserved. No part of this publication may be reproduced or transmitted in any form or by any means, electronic or mechanical, including photocopying, recording, storage in an information retrieval system, or otherwise without the prior written permission of the developer, unless specifically permitted under the Australian Copyright Act 1968 as amended.

National Library of Australia Cataloguing-in-Publication entry:
Ally's Mum
Morning Circle Story Time

ISBN 978-0-6450641-8-6

Typeset in Ciscopic
Images by ItsOkAlly and assets from Freepik.com

Made with love and thanks to:
Mothers and Marketers

MORNING CIRCLE STORY TIME!

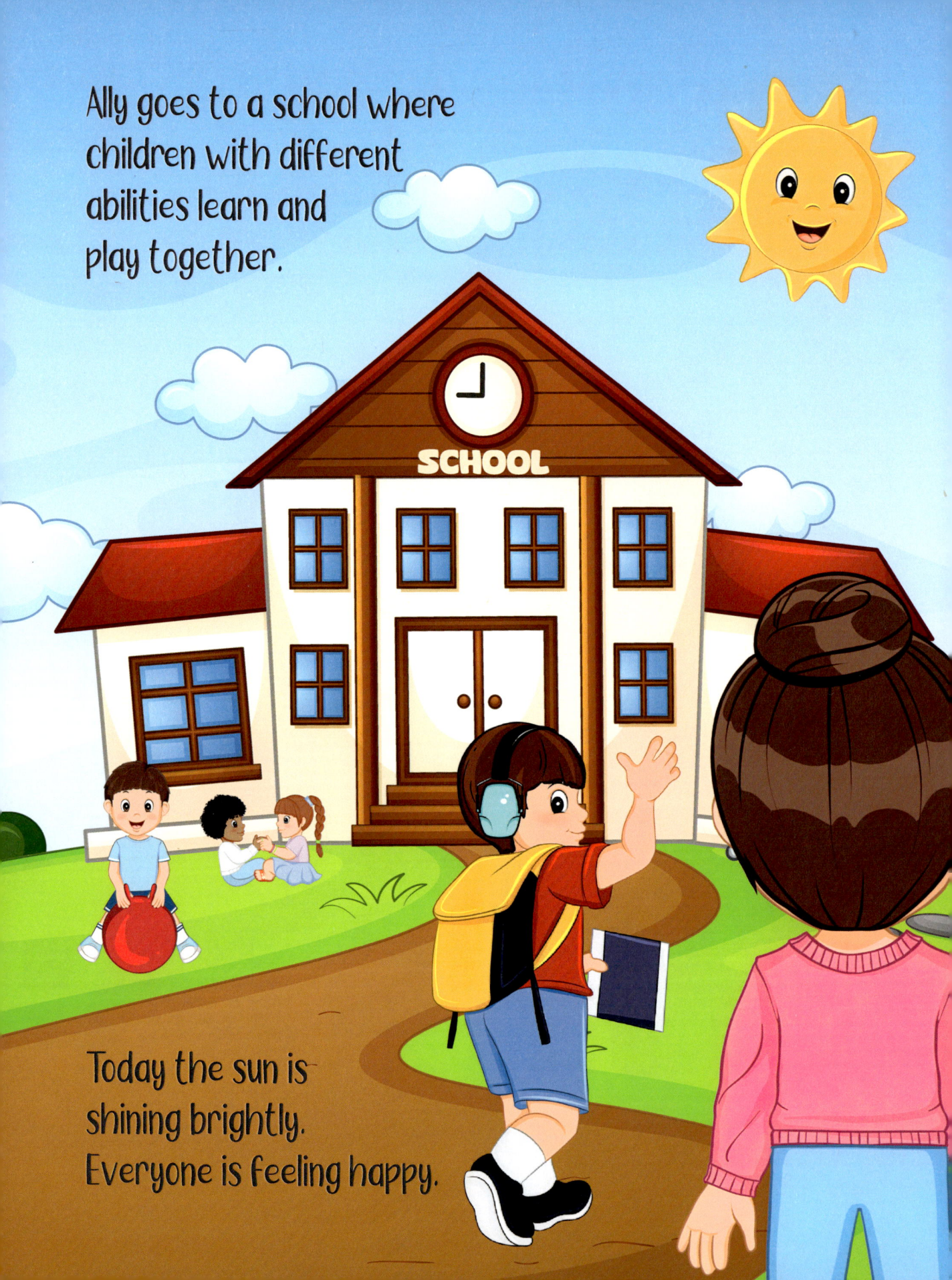

Every morning, some of the children gather in a circle to share their exciting adventures. Ally loves listening to his friends talk about all the fun things they did.

Today the teacher wanted to show them something special. Ally had brought an iPad to show pictures of his own adventures.

The children thought it was amazing and they were keen to share their stories after Ally shared his.

The teacher held up the iPad and described the picture. "Look, Ally went to the pond and fed the ducks. Seven cute little ducklings are following their mother out of the water with a splash," she said. She then pressed sound and the ducks quacked!

The children were delighted. They wanted to go on an adventure to the pond too!

Derek raised his hand with a big smile. "I played on my trampoline in the garden with my mother. We bounced up and down and laughed a lot!" He said.

Ally's eyes sparkled with delight as he imagined jumping on a trampoline too.

A girl with her hair in a ponytail spoke shyly. Her name was Penelope and she was new to the group. "I went to the park with my grandparents and swung high on the swings. It felt like I was flying in the sky!"

The children smiled. They understood Penelope's story and wanted to swing just like her.

Another girl, Sonya, put up her hand. She was holding an orange skateboard.
"I went skateboarding with my big brother. We zipped and zoomed down the street, feeling the wind in our hair!"

The children's eyes widened with wonder as they thought about skateboarding. They imagined themselves gliding along with their arms out, oh what fun!

Connor has been in the group as long as Ally has, but he's much better at talking to the others.
"I played basketball with my friends after school yesterday. We dribbled the ball and shot hoops. It was so much fun!" Connor said.

Ally thought about shooting a hoop and some of the children clapped. They loved the excitement of the game.

It was Spencer's turn. Ally and Spencer were good friends. "I went swimming in the pool. The water felt cool and refreshing. I moved my arms and had a ring to help me float. It was fun" Spencer said.

Everyone loved playing in water and they laughed and some children clapped their hands. They all wanted to go swimming at once!

Sammy put up his hand.
"I built a teepee out of sticks with my brothers. We tied the sticks together at the top. Then we wrapped a sheet around the sticks and took turns sitting inside. It was so much fun!" He said.

Everyone was excited by the thought of building a teepee. They all wanted to see it.

It was Ella's turn. "I went into the city with my Dad to see fireworks. There were lots of colours and sparkly lights high up in the sky and loud bangs and fizzes too."

The children loved fireworks and wished they could have been there too, it sounded so exciting!

Jayne said, "I picked a big basket of flowers with my Grandma. Then we made a daisy chain out of the flowers and wore them around our necks like jewels.

The children smiled, imagining all those pretty flowers made into necklaces.

Jack smiled and said, 'I caught a bus with my Dad and we got off at the cake shop and bought a big cupcake each. Mine was butterscotch with silver icing and little balls on top. It was delicious!

Everyone licked their lips, dreaming about that delicious cupcake.

Maddy put up her hand.
"I went to the beach and built a sandcastle in the sand. It had a flag on top and a moat around the outside. I collected shells and made it look pretty.

All the children loved building sandcastles in the sandpit at school. They started thinking about ideas for the next one they would build.

Arlo had been waiting patiently. The teacher asked him if he would like to share his adventure. "I went to a special school for dogs where they learn to help people. There were dogs and puppies everywhere! Then a lady came up and asked me if I wanted one all for myself! His name is Buddy." He said.

Arlo's father came in with the dog. The children were thrilled and had such fun playing until Arlo's father said it was time to take him home for a sleep. They all waved goodbye.

Everyone thought this was the best morning circle story time ever!

www.ingramcontent.com/pod-product-compliance
Lightning Source LLC
Chambersburg PA
CBRC092340290426
44109CB00008B/171